Wuthering Symphony

PUBLISHED BY

POETRY WORLD ORG

www.poetryworld.org

First Edition : 2020

ISBN - 9789389959055

Printed in India

Wuthering Symphony

Penned by

RUBAIA M. QUILL

ARIFUR RAHAMAN

ARIFUR RAHAMAN

Dedication of Wuthering Symphony

To Life who has given us some beautiful relations in the form of parents, siblings and friends and the emotions those relations create which have taken the form of art.

ARIFUR RAHAMAN

ABOUT THE POETS

A post-graduate in English literature and language, Rubaia Khatun started writing poetries at the age of twenty-two under her pen name Midnight Quill which after one year joined with her name, creating Rubaia M. Quill. Though, she never wanted to be a writer, her life journey and the nectar of emotions she received from her life inspired her to be one. She volunteers as a guide for various budding writers to help them in their writing journey. She also volunteers as a motivator/listener for an online community called PIAS (Project I am Strong). If she belongs from arts background, her brother, the other poet of Wuthering Symphony, Arifur Rahaman, belongs from science background and he is in the last year of his MBBS course. He started writing at the age of eighteen. Though at the beginning it was just a hobby, later it became his source of bringing out his voice and emotions. Both of them have co-authored books with Poetry World Organisation previously and this is their first solo book published by Poetry World Organisation.

ARIFUR RAHAMAN

INDEX

ARIFUR RAHAMAN

Birth of Life

A wuthering cacophony is gliding gracefully in the winds
A prismic light is colouring the canvas of the ruins
Drops of crystal is dazzling the piercing light
And a melancholy Selene keeps waiting on a swing.

Soaring time and dawn's cozy scarlet comes to sight
they blend and embrace the Blackness of the night
Zeus is waiting patiently to meet his Helios
Along with Selene though over is the nite.

Call they the five elements with a sigh
Trying to unite the mighty emblems singing a lullaby
A bright light gets thrust upon the ruins and slowly
A sprouting green comes to life against the desolation as a Bligh.

//Midnight Quill//

Thought of a Night

Sshh...

Eyes close

And now listen...

A forlorn howling sigh

Whispering to it's heart's content

Amidst the tranquil black canvas

The dark's detrimental deadly truth.

Truth that skulks behind

dazzling daylight, unmasking

Solely at Night.

And the street lights (sigh)
Mutter and Murmur as
Solitarily they witness
bleeding ravening
Sights.

//Midnight Quill//

Scars

Have you seen my Scars?
They are all 'Hale and Hearty'
Hidden   deep inside.

I Devour the silent screams
of my bleeding heart,
Every moment
while they engulf my soul
within a dark abyss,
Every second.

But enough!
Not any more.
It's Time
To illuminate a twinkle
in this abyss
To adore the world
with my clotted heart.
To wear my scars
as my weapons.

No matter how much
piercing they are
No matter how much
crude they are

No matter how much
scarred they are...

They are my ornaments
gifted by my life and
I'll bedizen them
Forever.

//Midnight Quill//

First shower of rain

Soft winged pillows are smiling
as upon them golden glitters started sprinkling.
Bathing they are in the warm glow
while melting on the land is the snow.
Birds are gossiping their own symphony
and enthralled I stand, perceiving this magical synchrony.

C-r-a-c-k! An electrifying blue,
illuminating the sparkling pillows. Why? No clue.
Transpiring into a blend now they are
Strange! Neither black nor white, but Greyer.
Drip Drip Drop Drop! Drip Drop Drop!
Greyish crystals are bestowing life to the crop.

The soothing smell after the rain
is making me remember a burning pain.
The twilight is now kissing my unkempt hair
while my crystal drops kept beholding the eternal blàr.

//Midnight Quill//

Dawn of Mahalaya

The greyish night is blending

with the blooming orange of the dawn.

Slowly steadily.

Engulfing the orangish grey canvas

is some warm golden glitters that yawns.

One Two Three

Members of a bird's family

chirping, gossiping, gliding and

with a smile enjoying glittery bath.

Hidden is now the

greyness. A warm blue

canvas can be seen. Small

cotton balls are dancing happily with

the sparkling reddish golden tint.

Birds are playing hide and seek.

Swinging are the winds,

in an unknown rhythm.

And intertwining with the nature is

Mahalaya's hymn.

//Midnight Quill//

Monday Talkies

"Hate You! Hate You!
Ugh... I just can't stand You!
Bloody Hell! Why come You
Every week?   Why?"

ENOUGH!!

WHY HATE **ME**?

WHAT HAVE I DONE TO **YOU**?

YOU ARE THE ONE WHO   MADE

ME THE BEGINNING OF **YOUR**

WORKING DAYS.   THEN

WHY HATE **ME**?

WHY CURSE **ME**?

HAVE YOU EVER THOUGHT   IF

I STOPPED VISITING **YOU**?

WHAT WILL HAPPEN THEN?

THINK!!

THINK!!

IF I, MONDAY, RESIGNED

FROM MY JOB? SNATCH

ONE DAY AWAY FROM

EVERY WEEK OF YOUR LIFE?

WHAT WILL YOU DO?

THINK

THINK

THINK....

AND THEN HATE ME.

//Midnight Quill//

Touch

Five cracked fingers are touching me.
"Who?" Old I am.   My crumbled skin
is a barrier, not letting me to see.
But still.   I can feel the touch. The
rough fingers are caressing my scars.

This touch!
This warmth!
Felt it before I, too.
Yes! how can I forget this Touch?
One   Two   Three...
Ugh... lost the count
So many years have passed.
Feels like crossed a decade
I since embraced this Touch!

This exquisite rough touch was
once a small smooth soft touch.
Years passed   and the touch grew.
into a slender beautiful touch.
Again,   years passed.
But this time   a new unknown touch.
Blending with a fresh rosy fragrance
a warm bright touch enveloped me.
Every single day I felt the touch
painted with bluish ink.

Years passed   Again.
But suddenly stopped one day.
I waited   waited   waited...
So long... slowly enveloped me
A dusty broken fragrance.

Drop!   Drop Drop Drop!
Smudging the colours are
fresh water drops.
Of Her.
Of Mine.
And today again   we
Embraced.   But this time   we
Embraced our faint weak smile.
Embraced our crumbled roughness.
Embraced our dusty yet crystal memories.

//Midnight Quill//

Forbidden Love

They both were alike, yet different. First ray of Dawn
he was, she was the Last ray of Night.
Everyday they met but for a split second.

Days passed turning into years their split seconds blended together.
Defying laws, dreams they weave, Together, only to be shattered.
"Forbidden! is their blending.", the dark grey clouds declared.
But foolish clouds they were. Forgot the strength of Love.

Years passed again. Same vast canvas with grey bars, electric shocks is
in view. In View is Them.
Knotted, Together. faint bright
smiles, fingers intertwined as hum they, their blending love.

//Midnight Quill//

Halloween

Stripping off from my Halloween costume
I hit the bed, embracing the darkness.
Tick! Tock! Tick! Tock!
Ugh.. Lost the count.. tick tock!
Suddenly felt an urge
A craving to drink.
Throat.. very...dried throat. Wa-t-e-r.
Tre-mb-ling hands, I gra--bbed the bottle.
Gulp! Gulp! Gu-l-Yuck!!
A drink of weird taste it was.
Salty sweet soothing but
a pungent smell.
Smaaaashhh!! Shattered the glass bottle I.
Tint of golden street light glistening
on the glassy smithereens and
on the bloody flowy liquid.
Shocked! Surprised! "Shit! Damn!
Blood it was. So sorry! I threw you away.
Need to hunt you again."

//Midnight Quill//

Penning down of thoughts

Tick! Tock! Tick! Tock!
Birds singing with the clock.
Sun yawns with a bright smile
And I... pen down
my trickling tears
happily in rhymes.

//Midnight Quill//

Four days, Four Nights

Gone he was. Passed may be.. four days, four nights?
But for me. It is a very long time.
Along the sea shore beholding I, some serene sights.
Gone he was. Passed may be.. four days, four nights?
And I, with a smiling tear is burying my plights.
Fanning my burning embers to avenge him for his crime.
Gone he was. Passed may be.. four days, four nights?
But for me. It is a very long time.

//Midnight Quill//

Thought of a Night

The night is very dark tonight.
With a dangling serene silent sight.
Her words are lost in the vast canvas yet,
The lost words weave a magical tale to recite.

//Midnight Quill//

Blend

Night stands still
as silence beautifies it.
Yet, a melancholic tune of flute
breaks the tranquil root.
She injects her melancholy into the scarred silence
as throughout the sky wings a crazy fragrance.

//Midnight Quill//

Forgotten

I have forgotten something.
I can't remember it.
My heart is playing tricks.
My mind has lost it's memories.
But What?
(Sigh) It seems like
I have forgotten 'WHAT' I have Forgotten.

//Midnight Quill//

Sunrise

The east is weaving
blushing scarlet with grey.
The dawn is crawling
in from the horizon.
Flowers are waiting at the window.
Young flowers,   Old flowers
All are waiting... to
spread their fragrance.
Fragrance of life.
Fragrance of death.
Young flowers,   Old flowers
All are waiting... for
The sun to rise.
And after some time,
The sun yawns with a smile.

//Midnight Quill//

Lonely wood

A lonely wood among moor
Decks herself with
Exquisite wrinkles, daily.

Still, she portrays youth canvassing
raw soothing fragrance while
Golden Glitters glisten
her fluttering limbs.
Together, they embrace
the rhythmic dance of unseen
making young grasses wobble.

And as darkness crawls, flamboyant
Solitude beautifies into looming
shadow, sheltering some sprouting youth.

//Midnight Quill//

Gate

The gate opens every second
Sometimes hither.
Sometimes tither.
And every second
an Outsider
becomes
an Insider, only to
become an Outsider
Again, after a lifetime.

//Midnight Quill//

Haiku

the silence of Night
embraces and lulls to paint
her tales with our words.

//Midnight Quill//

Fallen Leaves

They are crumbled
They are broken
They die with a proud smile
They are like the Unsung heroes.

Dusty, brown and yellow.
Hard, crispy and shrivelled.
Sun-baked they are.
They are the fiery rebels.

"Fallen leaves!" Everyone says.
Clinging loosely to their mother,
Waiting they are.
Waiting... for the tickles of the breeze to
justify their name   and
Bestow their life to the newborns.

//Midnight Quill//

Tale of five best friends

She is the messenger
of bright glittery sparkles.
Blending herself with
fruity fragrance,
Painting herself with
lustrous golden,
she visits the garden.
Every year.

With a fury subdued
deep down waiting for
the time to uproar.
Once her blazing anger
dissipates and showers pearls...

Visits a rusty brown haired girl.
Trying to hide her
broken heart from
'Fallen' insults,
she paints her soul
with dirty yellow.

As her tears blend
with her creator, enters

a cold-hearted terror.
Her frost-bitten words
pierce every heart bestowing
a spine-chilling horror.
At night, she wails
howling screams as her
coldness numbs her pain.

Days passed by,
Passed by Time.
One day smiles a
ray of hopeful shine.

Melting the cold heart
Blunting the knife-like tongue
visits a vibrant youth.
She showers her
flowery wind and paints
the dull mundane canvas
with colours of love.

My friend!
This's the tale
of five best friends.
Different yet unique and
Together, they craft magic.
Depends upon each other
like relay race members.
They don't visit together

They don't leave together
Still, complete a cycle
Every Year.
For their beloved creator.

//Midnight Quill//

A World Without Words

A world
Without words
Ever thought
How it would be like?

Sshh... obviously a silent world.
A screaming, hovering, engulfing silence.
That will tear our souls apart
That will pierce our smashed hearts
That will compel us to wither in pain.

And we...
We will yearn.
Every day, Every night
Every moment of our life.

For words...
For all those words
Which now, are nothing but
some crappy nuisance to us.

//Midnight Quill//

Won't

My Soul will be with you
but my Touch won't.
My Memories will speak with you
but my Voice won't
My Love will be with you   Forever
but my Life won't.

//Midnight Quill//

Apocalypse

The world is dangling from a string
The lustrous green meadows are now
Dusty heap of sand
Beauty is now terrific and sublime
Veil is now on-trend
Mirror has lost it's courage
Far away... a bell is ringing
Dong! Dong! Dong!
A harsh melancholic sound is
creeping, crawling, crashing
And slowly...
ushering us towards the
Apocalypse.

//Midnight Quill//

One poem, two stories

Shining in the sand
Like a broken wand.
Yet, I breathe.
But sometimes, loneliness haunts me.
Then like a magic, the breeze caresses me.
The lonely anguish of mine melts down.
The breeze winks at me and says,
"I'll Love You, for Eternity."

//Midnight Quill//

Note: This is a reverse poem. After reading from top to bottom, please read again from bottom to top. Hope you'll find two different stories.

I see beauty in...

I see beauty in

The silence of a dark still night.

The tranquil silence let us hear

The beats of our heart.

The voice of our soul.

I see beauty in

The night street lamps.

Their mutterings try to reveal

The lurking truths of the

Lonely dark alleys.

I see beauty in

The spellbinding relationship of

The sun and the shadow.

The sun: a bright essence of Darkness.

The shadow: a dark essence of brightness.

I see beauty in

The dying embers in the ashes.

Dying yet Dazzling in her full beauty.

A feeling of Hope

Amidst the destruction.

//Midnight Quill//

One

One lonely noon.

One solitary reader in one coffee shop,

reading one romantic book and

thinking when she will write her own.

Suddenly someone entered,

Breaking the tranquil silence,

Humming a tune.

Her one & only 'one' heart

stopped for one moment.

Love at first sight?

Finally! Her 'own' love story.

And suddenly,

her bubble bursts, her only 'one' is

Kissed away

by some-one 'else'.

One heart is now into smithereens.

The lonely noon passed away,

the dark night is falling.

One street lamp muttered, One street lamp sputtered.

And as the lonely noon was bidding adieu,

her Destiny wrote one story.

Story with one beginning, no ending.

Story of 'One-sided Love'.

//Midnight Quill//

Not forgotten

Time heals everything.

But... do we really forget everything?

No!

The Sun of the Time just,

Casts a Shadow over our crestfallen Soul.

Our invisible but smiling scars

are just, Veiled by Time.

Our Darkness is Never Forgotten.

They very much stay with us,

Hidden But Alive and

'Not Forgotten'.

//Midnight Quill//

Nothing changes

Today I lost.

I lost my Smile, my Sorrows,

my Peace. My Soul.

The night has fallen long back. I didn't know when.

I came to my room and I startled.

The blend of light and darkness was painting shadows.

And in the mirror I saw a figure, Unknown to me.

All Alone.

It gave me a feeling of Angst.

I tried to hunt it in my...   Already Lost Memories.

But I couldn't.

So I walked past the Stranger.

I went towards the closed window and opened it.

A blowing wind kissed me.

Tears trickled down.

I stood there.

The blushing scarlet and the cozy tangerine
entangled with love.

And I realized, Nothing has changed.

The sun, the moon... the stars are still here

painted on their very own Canvas.

And I... I still Breathe. (Sigh)

//Midnight Quill//

Thank You

Amidst
the crowd of concrete,
the cacophony of deafening machines,
the hustle and bustle of robots,
I miss the lurking little beauties
Of Life.

The careless whisper of the night wind
The pride of the dry fallen leaves
The burnt-out ends of misty days
The thunderous applause of grey clouds
The rhythmic grasses
The orchestric passerines.
I really miss you all.
And Thank You!
Thank You to all beings
residing in this ship called Earth,
for crafting me who I am today.

//Midnight Quill//

Indian Army : A Symbol Of Pride

Somewhere in the darkest path
where sun fails to reach.
With Himalayas in the north,
Indian ocean in the south,
Bay of Bengal in the east,
Arabian Sea in the west.
Away from his home, away from his family,
With his hardened body
deprived of sleep.
He doesn't care that he is tired.
Trained all his life in brutal conditions
Day and Night.
This barren & desolate world is his home.
Where thousands of people fear to go,
He goes their all alone.
Those cold poisonous snakes whose sight give us a
throbbing heartbeat,
He makes those snakes his daily food.
He allows the taste of fear to motivate his action.
Killing those snakes is the only option, for him.
He's just a common soldier, whose ranks are
growing thin.
He gives us blankets to cover us in need,

Waving high to show we are still undefeated.
If we can't honour him, while he's here to hear the praise,
Then at least give him homage, at the ending of his days.
Perhaps just a simple headline, in the paper , that might say;
"OUR COUNTRY IS IN MOURNING,
FOR A SOLDIER DIED TODAY."

~Arifur Rahaman

"Golden Memories"

Those loving memories of our early ages,

'Our school days'

Roaming about in Corridor, more

Than being in class.

It seems like only yesterday

Now the years have been passed.

Remembering the days gone by,

Happy times and the sad .

Continuously gazing the teacher with a crush on her,

And eating those tasty food from 'kaka'

Weren't that much bad.

During classes You don't fancy

May be sporting a frown.

But Be careful ;

Your grades may go down.!

High school is certainly

a complicated condition.

Starts off like an Indian Idol audition

Right from wishing 'Good Morning'

to your teacher

You're instantly judged.

I didn't like chemistry at all in class.

But the trick is to enjoy

Those P-Block elements & Decane rings in class.

The one you don't like,

Are not that much injurious.

10 years solved question papers

Are life saviours for us.

School journey is near to its end,

Waving goodbye to each

Teacher and friend.

Making promises of 'to keep in touch'

Ending up after few years exclaiming;

'Hey bro, what's up!'

Remember to show,

your parents, your actual grades.

Just be honest to yourself,

And don't hide behind the shades.

High school was certainly complicated,

Unfortunately reached to its end.

Keep it real,

And finish your final mission

With flying colours.

~Arifur Rahaman

A Strange Relationship

There was a moment,

Not so long ago

A newborn cried for the first time.

As he stepped into a strange and an unknown world.

A man held him with certain strength.

As tears of confusion ran down the newborn's face.

The man's daily mission was to make

the newborn smile.

With his daily tired excited face

Office to home, home to office.

Be it 3:30AM when slumber envelops the man,

Or 12:00PM from his office,

He never became tired to make him smile.

Years came & went, and

the little boy was in his first year of middle school.

There were many days, when he

used to return from school with tears

which pierced the man's heart like a sad cold dagger,

But he would sit there and console

him until the little boy smiles.

Slowly time changed as he entered his teenage

And the little boy was no more a little boy but a matured teen.

Time passed by, slowly

the kid started quarelling with his own father,

Who tried his best to keep his little son happy

all the time.

But that kid may have forgotten everything by now, as

innocence started trading with experience.

But in between all those quarrels, the

kid's love for his father didn't reduce.

It's just that he never expressed his love in front of his father

But, felt when he was out of his sight.

The kid is now a matured adult with all lavish lifestyle.

Got married few years after with a beautiful girl of his kind.

With his ongoing busy schedule & luxurious lifestyle

He forgot that his father is also growing old.

But that once newborn is matured enough now,

that made all the difference.

And so made up mind to shift to another country

to make his luxurious life more luxurious,

Leaving his aged father all alone.

The once newborn is now father of a newborn,

and repeated the same with his newborn son

Like the way his father took care of him.

And the day came,

His own son made up mind to send him old age home,

And, it was that time,

he realised what he did with his aged father years back,

But can't do now except regretting,

It's really late.

~ Arifur Rahaman.

Falling Apart

Its being 20 years of my life, & I've seen more than enough,

I've made it through the darkest nights,

where I just wanted to die.

I accept am not perfect.

But,

Will I be ever good enough?

Most likely not.

I'm not the perfect Islam.

I don't take communion.

I'm not a perfect son.

Not a perfect friend, nor a perfect lover.

Even am not a perfect student,

I can't do public speaking

I can't talk to people, I can't open up my mind,

I fear to share, so I keep everything bottled up.

The demons there will never leave me. But; I've

Something stronger

Hope & will power heals eternal misery.

Some says relationships can't heal you.

I've to disagree with that,

My relationship with the God,

is the ultimate remedy.

~Arifur Rahaman.

Real Close Friend ; My Sister

A sister isn't just a sibling.!

She's a whole world.

To look into my sisters' eyes & know,

What she's is thinking isn't a miracle,

It's natural .

To see her smile, to hear her talk,

Warms my heart ,

Soothes my soul.

To feel her heartbeat in me is special.

Fun house water fight, remember I do

Playing with mud pies,

Eating up chalk, paper ; I remember.

We've grown out of them ,

Yet we've not grown apart.

Sometimes we don't get along,

There are even times we fight

But I know you are always there,

You'll always care.

You were always there

and most part you've always been fair.

You've always shown support for me,

When everyone was doubting on me.

You always believe in what I do

So just know, I Love You.

You sympathise me, because you've been there,
It's comforting.

When you shares your dreams with me,

It's encouraging.

When you beats me up, because am a brat, It's learning.

My love for you, shall never expire,

To be like you, I always aspire.

One day together, we shall retire,

You're my big sister, I'll always admire.

I'm proud of you, and I know,

I can expect more good things from you

You aren't so far away from me

But it doesn't means that I don't miss you

So the next time I visit,

You'll see the new me.

This is just a small way to tell ;

I Love You.

~ Arifur Rahaman.

Thrashing Oneself

Hiding behind the dark shadow,

Trying to stay out of light.

Hoping no one will notice,

They've had yet another fight.

Restless mind everyday,

Tears turned dry.

I fear the bright light

I fear their faces.

Now,

Am afraid of everything, but can hide it well.

Can tuck the fear inside me whole day, but with a frenzied brain at night.

If you were to ask, how I am.?

I would rather smile & say, "She is Fine."

A depressed state of mind,

Discovering myself is the hardest rhyme.

I drown in high & low tides,

Can't win against the restraining pain within.,

My blood dries thin.

It's the time to hide in an encase,

letting the waves of my heart

crush against every thoughts

driving me insane

Not to become a butterfly

Not to fly in the bright light.

rather I'll build a leaf house,

& hide in there.

Until, I die

Or ,

Until you find me.

~Arifur Rahman

Backstabbers

Eyes shining like diamonds

All so innocent,

So pure,

Strolling around with style & grace.

Ah, that's just one side,

Just one face.

Your words are ambidextrous.

You use your words to feel good.

You augmented the situation ,

And now there's no affiliation .

They talk to my face

As happy as they can be,

Hiding a side ,

That no one can see.

Observe more closely ,

Look hard and watch

There's no beautiful soul .

But just two faced backstabbers.

Why are people so mean?

Why do people judge?

We all are same ,

But they are just to impress.

They don't know what else to do,

But just insult, laugh & to bitch behind us.

World is full of two face people

It's not a good thing

But what can we do?

~Arifur Rahaman

"Meri Maa"

You brushed my hair, tucked me in,

Made me laugh for hours on end.

You kissed my forehead whenever I stepped out

Ma, you never let me down.

I still remember those days when I was kid,

You used to play hide & seek.

You held my hand every time as I walked through the doors.

Ma, there's quite no one like you.

You listened to me talk about the fights.

Then you taught me how to handle it calmly.

You spoke with wisdom & of things you know.

You love to hear from me, 'Ma, I Love You.'

Times when I fought with you,

You cry in silent locking yourself in room

& again I'll cry, running to you,

Whispering with a broken voice,

'Maa, am sorry. (hug)

You are the one who taught me about life

How not to fight & what is right.

You are the one who cares for me

You are my eyes that help me to see

You are the one who knows me best

When it's time to have fun, & time to rest.

You are the one who helped me to dream,

You are the one who understood me without my screams.

You are more than a mother to me

You are the greatest friend I know,

In your eyes I can see reflection of myself. You
share a love that knows no end

A love that knows no end.

You call me every now & then

I fail to receive the call giving a lie.

But, sometimes I feel scared,

thinking of that day,

When I'll call you, but from the other side

The phone will say, 'She is gone.'

and all of a sudden,

Home will be so empty without you.

But I'll just pray to god,

'Ma, stay with me forever, as long as possible.'

"I Love You Ma."

~ Arifur Rahaman.

Fake Generation

In a world full of darkness,

I stood out, all alone .

Without having any idea

am right, or they were wrong.

Their whispers seep through,

the wall vents,

the crackle in the phone,

the inch left underneath the bedroom door

'The fake normalcy.'

This generation is ruined

by the fake & the mean.

But there are some good ones

stuck in between .

They never care what's going on,

Just want to know & play along.

They'll tell you anything to show they care

But in the end they are never there .

They say , 'Don't Cry'.! "It's not a big deal."

'Be thankful for what you've got.'

But to me it's the little thing,

That really means a lot.

Sometimes I really wonder,

Lies hurt, break hearts & sometimes can just fix it too.

But life goes on, we learn from our mistake &
broken heart

But still repeats the same & gets hurt.

We try not to hurt each other but it doesn't always
work

So, this is my promise

I'll always love you.

I promise.

~ Arifur Rahaman

The Dark Soul

I asked myself long before.,

'Should I write again?'

My soul answered -

That never again would I write

no more,

because I only felt Darkness.

Sitting in the cold dark corner

In the back of my room

It speaks to me

Saying, *I'm coming for you.*

Tears continue to pour.

I started fading away.

What was once bright,

Now turned dark...

My soul?

Another night closes in,

Darkness descends down.

Smothering, suffocating

Drowning me once again.

The corner keeps talking

About how am going to die.,

All I can do there is

Lie & cry.

I search my body for my soul,

But long back darkness has stole.

I pray but there's no site of light

I guess... Darkness is my friend...

The corner gets closer ,

Grabs me in.

The dark soul started burning ,

So does my skin.

Thinking ,

My bones shall lie there

Turning to dust,

Surrounded by an iron bed

Nothing but rust.

~Arifur Rahaman

Restart Button

Calm environment, clock making noise.
Anyone out there?
Anyone listening?
Words coming out but are silent
Tears flowing down, remembering memories
Mind screaming out loud.
No one out there
Fighting with the inner soul
Crying with all heart out, & a
Sudden light flash
Mobile glowing with a small message
"Will talk later."
after waiting for almost 24 hour.
Ignorance...
Calmness everywhere
Clock making noise, &
Pillow getting wet
& a thought
Kash mere life ka ek restart button hota.

~ Arifur Rahaman

We aren't Gods

Professional field.
Days of sleepless nights.
But, when finally landed here
So proud.
Happy with lots of hope.
We didn't know what was next.
Yes, we're budding Doctors.

Soon, misery came on us,
When we started Bio-chem!
Anatomy in Dissection Hall was fun,
But Microbiology hit us hard.
With Davidson & Bailey Luv
Taking away our sleep.

Midnight 2 and Maggi bowl,
Rooms getting decked up as DJ room.
Cold breezy terrace,
With a puff of cigarette,
Family with friends
Fighting with caterers,
Hostel life was really an amazing experience.

This is MBBS & we, the 'Students'
we learnt to Fear not, from the Fear.
To overcome hurdles to get success
Motivated, Inspired
Flexion, Supination
14 subjects, 9 semesters
The 50,000 pages concerto
White overcoat & stethoscope
5.5 years just passed by like flow of water
Only reason...
To save the soul who're still breathing.

Note from the poet: "Remember, Doctors aren't God and violence on Doctors are just brainless acts. We ignore our personal life to save those injured & sick patients. At the end of the day, if we lose a patient on OT table & due to other ailments, we also go through the same pain of not being able to save a life. Yeah, we can't afford to be emotional and get attached with those whom we treat with love and care and behave with them just as a patient, but Doctors do also have a heart. We're also human being... like you. Life and Death is not in our hands. We aren't Gods."

~Arifur Rahaman.
(MBBS, Final Year)